A WALK IN THE WOODS
Coloring Book

Dot Barlowe

DOVER PUBLICATIONS, INC.
Mineola, New York

Introduction

Not all of us are lucky enough to live in the countryside, where we can go walking every day through the woods on the other side of the meadow. But we all know the pleasures of nature—the glory of a new spring day, the elation of the first crisp days of autumn when the trees are turning red and gold, and the ticklish surprise of the first lacy snowflakes of winter landing on our collars. And yet there are some aspects of the seasonal changes that most of us give little thought to: just exactly what is happening to the plants and animals as those changes take place within the boundary of the woodland, under that magnificent crown of treetops we take so much for granted.

As is true in various ecosystems throughout the natural world, there are always some animals that prey on others. To humans, this sometimes seems sad or cruel.

Though we are members of a violent species and most of us are meat eaters, we somehow prefer to identify with gentle, soft-eyed herbivores like rabbits and white-tailed deer. But nature is a self-regulating system, and the predators have just as important a part to play in it as their prey. Without such a system, the landscape would become barren and still.

This book will supply some of the answers about how life depends on life and will show you how a walk in the woods on a fine spring morning (or any time at all!) can answer even more questions and at the same time reward you with some delightful surprises. So venture, but quietly, into the woodland, camera in hand, and you will be surprised at Nature's intricate handiwork that awaits you there.

Note: We have provided scientific species or genus names for most of the plants and animals we have encountered in our walk through the woods. But a few of them (including millipedes, termites, bark beetles, sow bugs, puffballs, slime mold, damselflies, and dragonflies) are representatives of whole classes or orders, and for those we have given only their common names.

Bibliographical Note

A Walk in the Woods Coloring Book is a new work first published by Dover Publications, Inc., in 2003.

International Standard Book Number

ISBN-13: 978-0-486-42644-0
ISBN-10: 0-486-42644-0

Manufactured in the United States by Courier Corporation
42644010   2014
www.doverpublications.com

Walking through the woods on a warm, fragrant April day can reveal a secret world where animals, plants, and insects are awakening to their never-ending cycle of life.

In the meadow before the woods, a **woodchuck** (*Marmota monax*), who woke recently from a long hibernation, enjoys the mild sunshine and the tender new grass shoots. His fur is a rich brown streaked with grayish hairs, and he may grow to more than two feet in length. In front of him, a spectacular

mourning cloak (*Nymphalis antiopa*), one of the season's earliest butterflies, floats lazily beside a **dandelion** (*Taraxacum officinale*). The mourning cloak's maroon wings are bordered in creamy yellow and sparked with electric blue spots. The trees looming in the background are still bare, although some of the **willow** (*Salix* spp.) branches have turned a light yellow-green and there is a pinkish haze where the fattening tree buds are showing signs of life.

As we enter the woods, the gleaming white petals of the **bloodroot** (*Sanguinaria canadensis*) at the bottom left and the reddish violet flowers of **hepatica** (*Hepatica* spp.) at left center catch our eye. They will soon be joined by other beautiful spring blooms—which will die back as the burgeoning leaves on the trees prevent the sun from warming the woodland floor.

In the near distance, a swampy pond is already bordered by the bright green leaves of **skunk cabbage** (*Symplocarpus*

foetidus), whose foul smell is perfume to the insects that pollinate it. A gentle movement among those leaves may prove to be tiny toadlets trying their land legs.

Closer at hand, a furtive rustle in the leaves turns out to be an **eastern chipmunk** (*Tamias striatus*)—reddish brown, with a dark stripe down his back, black and white stripes on either side, a white underside, and a dark tail. He focuses his black, white-bordered eyes on us a moment, then flees beneath the roots of a maple tree.

As the path leads closer to the pond, a sweet sound reminiscent of sleigh bells grows louder—the mating calls of the **spring peepers** (*Hyla crucifer*). Their song is lovely, but they are very hard to find. They are tiny, only an inch or so long, with gray-brown crosses on pale tan backs. Their feet have sticky pads on each toe, enabling them to adhere to the surfaces of water plants and reeds. With their throats swelled to bubbles that rival their length, their symphony reaches a frantic crescendo as darkness falls.

Larger and more noticeable is the beautiful light-brown **wood frog** (*Rana sylvatica*) with her conspicuous black mask. Before the ice was completely melted, she left her eggs in the bottom of the pond to hatch into tadpoles. During the warm weather she may go far from the water as she hunts through her woodland domain for insects and worms.

However lovely it may be for humans, for a bird his song is mostly a matter of letting others of his species know that the territory is taken. The spring migration brings in the males of most species first, and each male tries to find a place that is safe and that has plenty of food. Attracting a mate is next on the agenda, and if he succeeds, the female will usually proceed to build a nest—with the occasional help of her mate.

The **American robin** (*Turdus migratorius*) who's built her nest in the **dogwood tree** (*Cornus* spp.) at upper left has a russet breast, black head, and grayish wings and tail. The dogwood, now sporting white blossoms with greenish-yellow centers, will provide some protection from hawks and crows who favor young nestlings in their diet.

Below, to the right of the **pink lady's slippers** (*Cypripedium acaule*) at lower left, a brown-marked **house wren** (*Troglodytes aedon*) plucks an insect from a **blue violet** (*Viola* spp.). To the right of these violets are a few **white violets** (also *Viola* spp.). Behind them, growing behind the

4

root of the oak tree at center, is the pink-flowered **trailing arbutus** (*Epigaea repens*). At the lower right a **yellow-throated warbler** (*Dendroica dominica*), notable for its black mask and bright yellow throat and belly, brings small insects to its hungry youngsters in a nest hidden in the undergrowth.

If they have different feeding habits, several species of birds may occupy the same area. The zebra-backed, red-headed **red-bellied woodpecker** (*Melanerpes carolinus*), peering out from the oak tree at the center, eats grubs and beetles from under tree bark, and is no competitor for a robin, which eats worms. The woodpecker is looking out towards a snow-white dogwood in the distance. The shrub below the woodpecker is a pinky-white **mountain laurel** (*Kalmia latifolia*), and at the right center is a white-flowered **mayapple** (*Podophyllum peltatum*).

Even after a tree has fallen, it still plays a vital role in the forest ecology. As it decays, it provides homes and nutrients for all sorts of plants and animals.

The bright-orange, yellow-spotted **eastern newt** (*Notophthalmus viridescens*) at lower right is mostly nocturnal and feeds on earthworms and insects. It shares its hideaway with the pale gray **masked shrew** (*Sorex cinereus*) to the left, which has a ravenous appetite for larvae, spiders, and slugs.

The **maze fungus** (*Daedalea* spp.) in the middle of the log is yellowish white, and the small **cup mushrooms** at top right are bright red with white stalks. The **puffballs** at the lower right are white, and those at the top left are brown. The **coral mushrooms** (*Ramaria* spp.) on the bottom left are pale yellow. The patches of **slime mold** above them on the log are dark yellow.

The magnified creatures at top, all of which make their homes in rotten logs, are (from left to right) a **millipede**, a **termite**, a **bark beetle**, and a **sow bug**.

Almost summer, and in the woodland beyond the marshy pond, a **white-tailed deer** (*Odocoileus virginianus*) feeds cautiously in a small area of fresh green grass, her ears cocked for any unusual sound that will set her to flight. But there is more to her uneasy behavior—she has hidden a pair of tiny, white-spotted fawns beneath the protective fronds of **sensitive fern** (*Onoclea sensibilis*) and behind a **trillium** (*Trillium* spp.), which is instantly recognizable by its three-petaled white flowers. The fawns lie absolutely still, and their brown

and white coloration blends perfectly with the dappled sunlight under the ferns.

In our woodland there are no predators large enough to bring down a fawn, much less a full-grown deer, but dangers still exist. The fawns will need their mother until they are old enough to be on their own—about a year. In times of danger, their mother will try to lure predators and hunters away by bounding off from where the fawns are hidden.

7

This **northern oriole** (*Icterus galbula*), feeding her young in a hanging nest of dried grasses, string, or yarn on the branch of a maple tree, has a black head, yellow-orange body, and black-and-white wings.

The tree she uses to support her nest is full of little miracles. In late spring, as the weather warms, tiny leaflets, protected all winter by an outer husk, emerge to begin their growth. By midsummer they will have fully grown, forming a canopy over all the shade-loving plants that lie below. Trees are great wonder-workers. They absorb tons of water through their root systems and supply our planet with the very elements all life needs to exist, in the form of carbon dioxide and oxygen, as they exhale water vapor into the atmosphere.

The leaves seen in close-up are (left to right, top to bottom) **hickory** (*Carya* spp.), **beech** (*Fagus* spp.), **birch** (*Betula* spp.), **sugar maple** (*Acer saccharum*), **white oak** (*Quercus alba*), and **sweetgum** (*Liquidambar styraciflua*).

In a deep hollow under a maple's roots, a female **red fox** (*Vulpes vulpes*), having sent her mate away, has borne four pups, and now, three months later, they use the foot of the tree as their playground. Their coats have changed from the soft gray of infanthood to the reddish gold of approaching adult life; their eyes, once baby-blue, have become a golden yellow with the vertical, elliptical pupils of the fox tribe. Their mother has weaned them, and now she hunts constantly, scouring the woods for mice and voles, making sure her pups are well fed. The male fox, accepted back into the fold, provides them food as well. The den under the maple is a lively, noisy place filled with yapping, barking, and whining.

Above the den, helping to camouflage it, is a spreading mountain laurel with pinkish-white blooms, and in the foreground is a small stand of **yellow lady's slippers** (*Cyprideum calceolus*), each with a bright-yellow lip and narrow, purplish-brown petals

By late spring, many young animals have made their way into the world, and their mothers use clever tricks to keep them hidden. In a small rocky overhang there might be a darkened den containing a threesome of young skunks, and the grass not far from where we walk might conceal a nest of sleeping baby rabbits.

A mother **eastern cottontail** (*Sylvilagus floridanus*) may only nurse her four-inch babies twice a day, but before she leaves them she carefully scrapes grass and twigs over their grassy nest to camouflage it. Plenty of owls, foxes, snakes, and other predators would be happy to secure a meal from an unattended nest.

Baby rabbits are born blind and hairless, but within a week they will have developed a coat of fine brown hair and their eyes will be nearly open. And in only about sixteen days, the little ones will stop nursing, start eating greenery, and strike out on their own.

In the summer, sunlight speckles the dark forest floor around us, and the pond has grown a shock of tall reeds and **yellow iris** (*Iris pseudacorus*), along with white-flowering **fragrant water lilies** (*Nymphaea odorata*). Bird calls are few at this season; the burgeoning insect population gets most of the bird's attention.

Along the path, such wildflowers as the brilliant red **cardinal flowers** (*Lobelia cardinalis*) in the right foreground, the yellow-orange **day lilies** (*Hemerocallis fulva*) at left center,

and the sweet-smelling yellowish-white **honeysuckle** (*Lonicera* spp.) in the left foreground have come into their own. Patches of three-leafed **poison ivy** (*Rhus radicans*) and five-leafed **Virginia creeper** (*Parthenocissus quinquefolia*) twine their way up the trees to the right.

Many small furry creatures are asleep during the day, but as we walk we see two squirrels foraging on the woodland floor and a pair of chipmunks playing tag on the poison-ivy tree.

All but two of the robin's four nestlings made it into summer. And now, short of tail, with speckled, pale-russet breasts, the youngsters search for worms hidden under the wet leaves left by last night's rainfall. The abundance of earthworms has also brought out an extraordinary creature—a **marbled salamander** (*Ambystoma opacum*) sitting in a puddle, somewhat camouflaged by his blackish-gray body with silvery white crossbands. He hasn't wandered too far from the pond—just far enough to supplement his diet of small bugs.

Behind him, where the **forget-me-nots** (*Myosotis sylvatica*) bloom in pale-blue profusion, a **damselfly** alights momentarily after flitting back and forth across the water on iridescent wings, and a pair of **painted turtles** (*Chrysemys picta*) lie placidly sunning themselves on rocks at the pond's edge, until hunger or the midday sun will drive them back into the water.

Today we are in luck! After skirting the pond, we find that the snow-white, yellow-centered flowers of the **common strawberry** (*Fragaria virginiana*) have attracted not only bees but also an **eastern box turtle** (*Terrapene carolina*). Although he will have to be satisfied with nibbling leaves and flowers now, he will be back later this season to feast on the delicious wild strawberries. The turtle's carapace (shell)—dusky brown splashed with a brilliant yellow-orange design—protects him so well that

he may live to be 100 years old if his habitat is left undisturbed.

Behind the wild strawberries, curled in a spot of sun on a rocky outcrop, is a cream-colored, red-and-black-marked **milk snake** (*Lampropeltis triangulum*)—a rare find, because he usually comes out only at night. Like all snakes, he plays an important role in keeping the rodent population from taking over our food supply. He sometimes also eats other snakes—including poisonous ones.

Twilight, and the red fox vixen rouses her fast-growing pups and nudges them into following her on their first hunting expedition. They tag after her eagerly, in single file. In the darkness away from their familiar haunts, they crowd their mother as she moves to her favorite hunting ground.

Foxes will eat anything that seems a good meal, even carrion, but they prefer to do their own hunting. It is unlikely that the young foxes will capture anything tonight, but their mother is a seasoned hunter. She leads them to an errant **white-footed mouse** (*Peromyscus leucopus*) trying to hide under a log, pounces on it, and drops it at their feet.

Many lessons will follow this one, and by the end of summer the fox pups will have become familiar with all the wary, intelligent ways that foxes need to survive in a world with hunters, dogs, and devastating changes in habitat.

If you chance to walk in the woods at night, you might be surprised by something that goes "bump in the night." An **eastern screech owl** (*Otus asio*), protecting its nest in a tree above you, might take a swipe at your face or head to let you know whose territory you have just violated. A fierce night-time hunter, it searches the woods on silent wings for mice and insects in order to feed its three to eight offspring—to say nothing of its own ravenous appetite.

The call of this 10-inch, yellow-eyed, brown-streaked owl is a quivering wail that slowly peters out—a frightening thing to hear if you are alone in the dark woodland. Superstitious people used to say that the screech owl's call meant someone was going to die. But in fact this owl bodes evil for nothing except destructive insects and rodents and is a benefit to farmers in the area. Its sad, pitiful wail is merely a way to inform its beloved of its presence.

We have discovered a delightful meadow in the woods, bordered by tall ferns, pinkish-purple wild **raspberry** (*Rubus* spp.) in the foreground, and thorny wild **rugosa roses** (*Rosa rugosa*) in the background. Feeding in this hidden place are the white-tailed doe and her two half-grown fawns. Their soft brown coats are still sprinkled with rows of white spots which will be gone in the fall.

Summer is a time of plenty for deer and other woodland creatures, and the fawns will grow to maturity unhampered and well fed. This warm, sunny spot is abuzz with bees and countless other insects, and the air fairly dances with butterflies. The **red admiral** (*Vanessa atalanta*) in the lower foreground, whose wings are black, red-banded, and spotted with white, is a friendly butterfly that might, if you stand still, land on your collar.

As we wander through the late-summer flowers, we notice a dark, fuzzy mass high on a branch above us—a drowsy **porcupine** (*Erethizon dorsatum*). Usually this large rodent sleeps during the day and is more active at night. But he does not have to go very far for food. Sleeping up in a tree gives him the opportunity of having breakfast, lunch, and dinner just a sniff away, because his favorite foods are twigs, buds, and the inner bark of trees.

Although the porcupine is gentle, he has an arsenal of weapons that he can use whenever he feels threatened. His quills, numbering perhaps 30,000, lie flat against his body beneath the long brown-black silky fur. They loosen at a touch and are extremely painful to remove.

A female porcupine will have only one baby in April or May. The baby porcupine can eat solid food and climb trees within a few hours of its birth, and it will spend the rest of its life among the trees.

Many of the small animals we have met on our walks live a precarious existence—threatened not only by foxes, skunks, raccoons, and the occasional weasel, but also by sudden death from above. A **red-shouldered hawk** (*Buteo lineatus*) such as this one may wait silently on a low branch to swoop down on frogs, rabbits, mice, and even insects.

The **common garter snake** (*Thamnophis sirtalis*) he has just caught is also a predator, which eats frogs, toads, sala-manders, earthworms, and occasional mice. Garter snakes are the most widespread snakes in the U.S. and can be found everywhere but the deserts of the Southwest. Their coloring varies by region. This one is dark olive, with a pale-yellow stripe on its back and a pale-yellow underside.

The red-shouldered hawk has russet shoulders and a russet breast striped horizontally with white. Its upper side is mottled black and white, and its eyes are golden.

Four months old and perfect replicas of their parents, this trio of young rabbits is out for a moonlight dinner. Cottontails are first-class vegetarians, eating grasses, berries, grains, and herbs of all varieties. The one at the right has found some raspberries, and the one in front is dining on **red clover** (*Trifolium pratense*).

Life is unbelievably perilous for these bright-eyed creatures, but rabbits are so prolific (producing four or five litters per summer) that a substantial number always manage to survive. At this age they are already quite wary of woodland dangers and will scramble for the underbrush at the slightest sound. The prowling weasel is their greatest enemy, but many other predators would like nothing better than a plump rabbit for dinner.

Their soft coats are medium brown with a touch of russet at the neck, and there is a bit of white encircling their liquid brown eyes.

In the autumn our woodland has become a grand bouquet of brilliant colors. The reds and yellows of the maples and russets and wines of the oaks glow against the dark green of an occasional stand of hemlock. In the deciduous trees, the green layer of food-producing chlorophyll has faded and left the leaves to revert to the colors that lie beneath—each species of tree true to its own coloration.

The gray-green pods of the **common milkweed** (*Asclepias syriaca*) are shaking out their silky white fluff on every breeze. Orange-and-black **monarch butterflies** (*Danaus plexippus*), once anchored to the undersides of the tough milkweed leaves as pale green-and-gold pupae, congregate in the brisk fall air and prepare to fly south for the winter.

Soon, with the cooler weather, the songs of the insects will be stilled. A few birds will remain in our woodland throughout the winter, but flocks of others have already begun their migration southward.

The eastern chipmunk in the foreground and the **eastern gray squirrel** (*Sciurus carolinensis*) behind him are both rodents, but they have different habits. The chipmunk is not very sociable. He spends most of his time on the ground and lives in an underground burrow, where he stores the nuts and seeds he has found. The squirrel, on the other hand, likes to play with other squirrels. He spends most of his time in the trees, but buries his booty in holes in the ground—which helps the forest, because some of the acorns and other seeds take root and grow into trees.

The chipmunk's coat is reddish brown, with a dark stripe down its back and black and white stripes on either side. Its underside is white, and its tail is dark. The squirrel has a soft gray coat with a white underside. Both animals have dark lustrous eyes ringed with white.

The **partridgeberry** (*Mitchella repens*) in the foreground is an evergreen creeper with brilliant red fruit.

The rustle of crisp fallen leaves beneath our feet, the brisk cool air, and the earthy smells of autumn make this October day seem rich with the promise of discovery. Almost hidden under the leaves at the foot of an oak tree is a bounty of autumn mushrooms. Their extravagant colors and sculptured shapes belie the fact that they are parasites, living on dead or dying plant life. In the woodland's ongoing chain of life, they have an important job: breaking down plant material for the chemical replenishment of the soil.

In our excitement about finding the mushrooms, we have almost missed seeing the fully antlered white-tailed buck standing perfectly still in the background. Suddenly, with a snorting whistle, he bounds off into the deep woods. Our presence has apparently frightened him—although with a full rack of antlers he is really full of fight, and any other buck who meets up with him today will have to be ready to do battle.

The **two-colored bolete mushroom** (*Boletus bicolor*) at lower left has a red-violet cap lined with pale yellow and a red-violet stalk. Next to the boletes are a cluster of poisonous **jack o'lantern mushrooms** (*Omphalotus illudens*), which are brilliant yellow-orange (and which glow in the dark). At top left, behind the stump, are two edible **parasol mushrooms** (*Lepiota procera*), which are whitish gray with brown scales. A **violet-toothed polypore** (*Trichaptum biflorus*), whitish with violet edges, is growing on the stump itself, and to the lower right of the stump is a light-yellow **coral mushroom** (*Clavaria* spp.). Below them are three vivid red **hygrophorus mushrooms** (*Hygrophorus* spp.). At the bottom right corner is a **jack-in-the-pulpit** (*Arisaema triphyllum*), whose fruit is glowing red.

In autumn, frogs and toads unerringly prepare themselves for hibernation—a state of semilife that will enable them to survive the winter.

Frogs such as the **pickerel frog** (*Rana palustris*) at the left will dive beneath the surface of the pond and bury themselves in the mud and leafy debris for the long sleep. Unless the pond freezes to its very bottom, which is unlikely, their skin will absorb enough oxygen from the water to keep them alive until spring.

Toads, which have spent most of the summer on the woodland floor, will dig down three feet or so to hibernate below the frostline, as this **American toad** (*Bufo americanus*) has done. There they will stay until their inner clock informs them that warmer weather has returned.

The pickerel frog is pale brown with a yellow-tinged white belly and blackish spots on its back. The American toad is primarily olive or black with hints of rusty red.

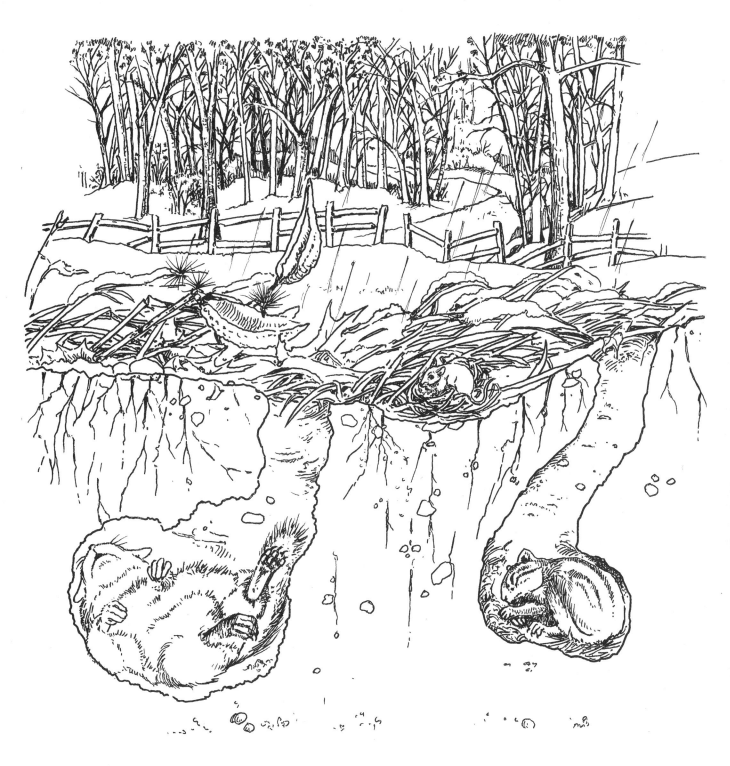

On this gray, bone-chilling December morning the temperature hovers below freezing. Light snow has begun to filter down, making our path even more slippery as we walk over the fallen leaves. We see little greenery except an occasional mountain laurel or other evergreen and perhaps a remnant of a summer vine peeking from beneath the snow. Empty, brownish-gray milkweed pods stand in grotesque shapes, some leaning on the stiff, withered meadow grass and others caught in the remnants of long-gone asters. Most of the

deciduous trees are bare, though the oaks still hang on stubbornly to some of their brown rustling leaves.

Underground, near where we walk, a woodchuck hibernates, warm in his burrow. So do half-sleepy chipmunks, who will waken every so often to eat. If we are in luck, we may get a glimpse of a reddish-brown white-footed mouse, who stays active all winter—but on a day like this she may decide to stay home in her nest.

The pond where the spring peepers trilled their first song is edged with ice and now holds only brittle, broken reeds and dead iris leaves. Beneath the water and ice, however, is a colony of gray-brown tadpoles and almost transparent **dragonfly** larvae that will survive the winter in deep pools along with the frogs buried in the leafy debris and fish such as these **bluegills** (*Lepomis macrochirus*) that feed on insect larvae.

Winter will be less of a struggle for these underwater creatures than for some of the animals that live on the land.

The bluegill, a member of the sunfish genus, is olive green above with blue sides shading down to a red-orange underside. Its face has two blue markings running back from the mouth to the gills.

The three **white-throated sparrows** (*Zonotrichia albicollis*) at right foreground and center have joined a trio of **purple finches** (*Carpodacus purpureus*) in the middle background to feast on seeds shaken loose by the wind. The sparrows have brownish backs, grey breasts, and a yellow spot on the forehead; the male finch is dull red, and the female is brown-striped. A pair of **black-capped chickadees** (*Parus atricapillus*), center, and their cousin, a **tufted titmouse** (*Parus bicolor*), behind them, arrive next; all three sport dove-gray backs and pale chestnut-and-white undersides. Shortly thereafter, a brilliant splash of red signals the coming of a **northern cardinal** (*Cardinalis cardinalis*) and his lady in buff-brown plumage with an yellow-orange bill.

Suddenly, with a shriek and a flurry of blue and white, a **blue jay** (*Cyanocitta cristata*) disperses this little mob. After he has settled down to eat, the smaller birds return one by one.

Beyond the partially frozen pond where an **American crow** (*Corvus brachyrhynchos*) has taken up a temporary perch, a group of white-tailed deer are browsing on the twigs remaining on the trees and shrubs that have already been grazed by other members of their family. Some have even nosed under the snow for the dried grasses that lie beneath.

Food is hard to come by in winter, but now spring is only weeks away, and these does and yearlings will survive. Sometimes individual deer do starve—but that is Nature's way of ensuring survival for future generations of the species. Even the tapping away of a black-and-white **downy woodpecker** (*Picoides pubescens*) at the bark of an oak tree for grubs and small insects hiding there is Nature's way of controlling next year's insect population; it helps both the woodpecker and the woodland.

On a more distant oak, we again spy a sleeping porcupine. With his food source at the tip of his nose, he may not come down until spring.

It is March. The snow is finally melting, letting dark patches of the woodland floor show through, and life is beginning to stir. Now that the pond is free of ice, the sunshine sparkles brilliantly on its surface. The rounded tips of new skunk cabbage are rising out of the mud on the embankment, and bunches of hepatica leaves are popping up among the leafy debris. A pair of bright-eyed chipmunks are chasing each other over the trunk of a maple that fell in a winter storm.

Soon the woodchuck will be out to chew on the new grass outside his winter burrow, and at the edge of the meadow there are dandelion leaves and fat dandelion buds for him to look forward to.

It is still too early for the return of the migrating birds, but the sweet trill of a white-throated sparrow and the bell tones of a cardinal's courting song let us know that all is well in our woodland—and that throughout the spring we will have many chances to walk in the woods.

Common Names

arbutus, trailing 4–5
beech 8
beetle, bark 6
birch 8
bloodroot 2
bluegill 26
bug, sow 6
butterfly, monarch 20
butterfly, mourning cloak 1
butterfly, red admiral 16
cardinal, northern 27
cardinal flower 11
chickadee, black-capped 27
chipmunk, eastern 2, 11, 21, 25, 29
clover, red 19
cottontail, eastern 10, 19
crow, American 28
damselfly 12
dandelion 1
deer, white-tailed 7, 16, 22–23, 28
dogwood 4–5
dragonfly 26
fern, sensitive 7
finch, purple 27
forget-me-not 12
fox, red 9, 14
frog, pickerel 24
frog, wood 3
fungus, maze 6
hawk, red-shouldered 18
hepatica 2, 29

hickory 8
honeysuckle 11
iris, yellow 11
jack-in-the-pulpit 22–23
jay, blue 27
lady's slipper, pink 4–5
lady's slipper, yellow 9
laurel, mountain 4–5, 9
lily, day 11
maple, sugar 8
mayapple 4–5
milkweed, common 20
millipede 6
mouse, white-footed 14, 25
mushrooms 22–23
mushroom, coral 6, 22–23
mushroom, cup 6
mushroom, hygrophorus 22–23
mushroom, jack o'lantern 22–23
mushroom, parasol 22–23
mushroom, two-colored bolete 22–23
newt, eastern 6
oak, white 8
oriole, northern 8
owl, eastern screech 15
partridgeberry 21
peeper, spring 3
poison ivy 11
polypore, violet-toothed 22–23
porcupine 17, 28
puffballs 6

rabbit 10, 19
raspberry 16
robin, American 4–5, 12
rose, rugosa 16
salamander, marbled 12
shrew, masked 6
skunk cabbage 2, 29
slime mold 6
snake, common garter 18
snake, milk 13
sparrow, white-throated 27
squirrel, eastern gray 11, 21
strawberry, common 13
sweetgum 8
tadpole 26
termite 6
titmouse, tufted 27
toad, American 24
trillium 7
turtle, eastern box 13
turtle, painted 12
violet, blue 4–5
violet, white 4–5
Virginia creeper 11
warbler, yellow-throated 4–5
water lily, fragrant 11
willow 1
woodchuck 1, 25, 29
woodpecker, downy 28
woodpecker, red-bellied 4–5
wren, house 4–5

Scientific Names

Ambystoma opacum 12
Acer saccharum 8
Arisaema triphyllum 22–23
Asclepias syriaca 20
Betula spp. 8
Boletus bicolor 22–23
Bufo americanus 24
Buteo lineatus 18
Carpodacus purpureus 27
Cardinalis cardinalis 27
Carya spp. 8
Chrysemys picta 12
Clavaria spp. 22–23
Cornus spp. 4–5
Corvus brachyrhynchos 28
Cyanocitta cristata 27
Cypripedium acaule 4–5
Cyprideum calceolus 9
Daedalea spp. 6
Danaus plexippus 20
Dendroica dominica 4–5
Epigaea repens 4–5
Erethizon dorsatum 17
Fagus spp. 8
Fragaria virginiana 13
Hepatica spp. 2

Hygrophorus spp. 22–23
Hyla crucifer 3
Icterus galbula 8
Iris pseudacorus 11
Kalmia latifolia 4–5
Lampropeltis triangulum 13
Lepiota procera 22–23
Lepomis macrochirus 26
Liquidambar styraciflua 8
Lobelia cardinalis 11
Lonicera spp. 11
Marmota monax 1
Melanerpes carolinus 4–5
Mitchella repens 21
Myosotis sylvatica 12
Notophthalmus viridescens 6
Nymphaea odorata 11
Nymphalis antiopa 1
Odocoileus virginianus 7
Omphalotus illudens 22–23
Onoclea sensibilis 7
Otus asio 15
Parthenocissus quinquefolia 11
Parus atricapillus 27
Parus bicolor 27
Peromyscus leucopus 14
Picoides pubescens 28

Podophyllum peltatum 4–5
Quercus alba 8
Ramaria spp. 6
Rana palustris 24
Rana sylvatica 3
Rosa rugosa 16
Rhus radicans 11
Rubus spp. 16
Salix spp. 1
Sanguinaria canadensis 2
Sciurus carolinensis 21
Sorex cinereus 6
Sylvilagus floridanus 10
Symplocarpus foetidus 2
Tamias striatus 2
Taraxacum officinale 1
Terrapene carolina 13
Thamnophis sirtalis 18
Trichaptum biflorus 22–23
Trifolium pratense 19
Trillium spp. 7
Troglodytes aedon 4–5
Turdus migratorius 4-5
Vanessa atalanta 16
Viola spp. 4–5
Vulpes vulpes 9
Zonotrichia albicollis 27